ⓕUNFAX™

DINO DISCOVERIES

Written by Stephen Bowkett

ACKNOWLEDGEMENTS

The publisher would like to thank the following for their kind permission to reproduce the photographs:

MUSEUM SOURCES:
Natural History Museum, London
Sedgwick Museum
Yorkshire Museum
Royal Scottish Museum
Hunterian Museum
Royal Tyrrell Museum of Palaeontology, Alberta, USA
Staatliches Museum Für Naturkunde, Stuttgart, Germany

AGENCY:
Science Photo Library

MODELS:
Sue Donkin

ARTWORK:
Graham Rosewarne
Giuliano Fornari
Simone End

ADDITIONAL PHOTOGRAPHY:

Colin Keates
John Holmes
Kim Taylor
Geoff Brightling
Andy Crawford
John Downs
Harry Taylor
Karl Shone
Roby Braun

ⓕUNFAX™

Earth formed a little over 4.5 billion years ago, out of a cloud of gas and dust floating in space. As the particles in the cloud swirled together, gravity made the cloud collapse towards its centre.

The central part became the densest. Eventually, the heat and pressure in the middle became so great that it ignited in a great burst of radiation – and the Sun was born.

Other smaller swirls and eddies in the remains of the cloud that were orbiting the new Sun became the other planets of the solar system.

Earth's Position

Earth is the third planet from the Sun, at a distance of 150 million kilometres (93 million miles). That's just far enough away to allow water to exist as a liquid. This is important because all life on Earth, now and in the past, needs water to survive. Without it, neither we nor the dinosaurs could ever have existed.

Earth in the Triassic Period, when dinosaurs first appeared

ONCE, LONG AGO...

The last of the dinosaurs died out around 65 million years ago, at the end of a period of time known as the Cretaceous Period. The first dinosaurs appeared a long time before that, during the Triassic Period, around 225 million years ago. While modern humans have only been around for the last 100,000 years or so, dinosaurs ruled the world 1,600 times longer than that – for around 160 million years.

Socket-Toothed Creatures

By the time dinosaurs had evolved – from an even more ancient group of creatures called the thecodonts, meaning 'socket-toothed' – life itself had been on the Earth for nearly 3.3 billion years!

Euparkeria

Ocean Life

The earliest life consisted of simple, one-celled animals, which scientists think first formed from the rich mix of chemicals in the early oceans. It took a long time for tiny, individual cells to evolve into dinosaurs such as meat-eating Tyrannosaurus rex!

It is almost impossible to imagine the huge lengths of time involved in the history of our world, but to help with the task, scientists have given names to different eras, which chart the development of life from its first appearance on Earth.

PRECAMBRIAN ERA	millions of years ago		
Archaean – life began during this time	4500	–	2500
Proterozoic – life spreads in the seas	2500	–	570
PALAEOZOIC ERA (Ancient Life)			
Cambrian – life flourishes in the seas	570	–	510
Ordovician – first fish appear	510	–	439
Silurian – first plants appear on land	439	–	409
Devonian – amphibians appear on land	409	–	363
Carboniferous – first reptiles, plants flourish	363	–	290
Permian – reptiles flourish	290	–	245
MESOZOIC ERA (Middle Life Era)			
Triassic – earliest mammals evolve	245	–	208
Jurassic – the rise of the dinosaurs	208	–	146
Cretaceous – dinosaurs rule, followed by extinction	146	–	65
CENOZOIC ERA (New Life)			
Tertiary Period:			
Palaeocene – large mammals develop	65	–	55
Eocene – primates (apes) appear	55	–	38
Oligocene – primates evolve	38	–	25
Miocene – modern animals appear	25	–	5
Pliocene – man-apes appear	5	–	2
Quaternary Period:			
Pleistocene – earliest humans appear	2	–	0.01
Holocene – modern humans develop	0.01	–	–

THE EARLIEST LIFE

If you stepped back in time to the Palaeozoic Era, you would probably think that it was a pretty bleak place.

Standing on the shore of an ancient ocean, you would see only rock, mud and water. Perhaps active volcanoes would be erupting, and the sky would be churning with clouds. No plants would be visible, and no insects or dinosaurs...and certainly no birds or mammals. Everything that lived then lived in the seas – they were thriving places! Some scientists think that throughout the Palaeozoic Era, life 'experimented' with an enormous number of different forms.

Eryops skeleton

A Multitude of Creatures

Life evolved (developed) from one-celled creatures, to multi-celled organisms, such as jellyfish, worms, snails, crabs and other invertebrate animals (creatures without backbones) including trilobites (left). These formed one of the most successful groups of that time.

Trilobite

No one knows exactly how life first formed on Earth, but as soon as it appeared, it changed with each passing generation. This happened because of environmental changes, such as different climates, new predators and new places to live. Only the living things that can adapt to these changes survive. The babies of these 'survivors' will be a little bit different from their parents and even better at surviving. The changes are so small and happen so slowly that it takes millions of years to become noticeable.

Fight to Survive

Every different kind, or species, of plant and animal competes with many other species for food and territory. Only the 'winners' live to have babies that are a little bit different and even better competitors. This very slow, constant change from one generation to the next is called evolution. Over the course of billions of years, from the start of the Archaean Period, living things have been evolving. There were very simple creatures at the start, followed by more complex plants and animals in more recent times.

THE AGE OF FISH

Over tens of millions of years, simple one-celled organisms became more complex. They evolved into fish which swam in the seas.

Late Jurassic fish – vertebrate

Like fish today, they probably released thousands of eggs directly into the water. Most of the eggs, or the tiny hatchlings, would have been eaten by other creatures. It was the sheer number of eggs which allowed the species to survive.

Out For a Stroll

Some fish developed very muscular fins. An example is Eusthenopteron, whose powerful, lobe-like fins, plus its ability to breathe air directly from the atmosphere, allowed it to 'walk' short distances on land. Such journeys from one pool to another probably led to the development of the amphibians.

The first amphibians were still more at home in the water than on land. They appeared in a time called the Devonian Period, some time after the first land plants had evolved. They were called Tetrapodomorphs (four-footed shape). These creatures were the ancestors of modern-day amphibians, such as frogs and salamanders, which are just as happy on land as they are in the water.

Sensitive Skin

The skin of amphibians is moist and very sensitive to the heat of the sun, so those early amphibians needed to return to the water often, to avoid drying out. Also, amphibians need water to lay their eggs in. For both of these reasons they do not stray far from the edges of streams and ponds.

Amphibians Today

Today, we can see the typical egg-laying process of amphibians when we look at frogs, which lay their eggs in jelly-like clumps, then leave them to hatch into tadpoles which fend for themselves.

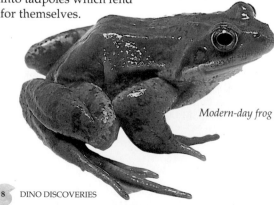

Modern-day frog

The Spread of Life
There are many advantages of living in the oceans.
Water can support the weight of large creatures,
and food is always plentiful. Also, the temperature
throughout the seas stays fairly constant – unlike on
land, where extreme cold can follow extreme heat.

Even so, the pressure on life to spread and vary
through evolution allowed early air-breathers, like
the fish Eusthenopteron, to evolve even further.

Leggy Fins
By the Carboniferous Period, creatures like
Ichthyostega had evolved. This was one of the first
amphibians. It had a long, strong, fish-like tail, but
the fins had developed into legs, which allowed it
to move and supported its weight on land.

Ichthyostega

True Air Breather
Like all amphibians, even those alive today,
Ichthyostega was probably more at home in water
than on land. It was a true air breather, but also
had gills like a fish. It would have been clumsy
on land, like a modern seal.

REPTILES ARRIVE

Reptiles are thought to have evolved from animals similar to Ichthyostega, but in a different way to later amphibians. They were more successful than amphibians when it came to colonising the land. This was for several reasons.

Scaly Skin...

The skin of a reptile is dry and scaly. Early reptiles' skin was not in such danger of getting damaged by the Sun as the amphibians' moist skin. This meant that reptiles could venture further from water, and were not so vulnerable when pools dried up.

...And Tough Eggs

Reptiles laid their eggs on land, and often covered them with sand or mud for protection. The eggs themselves were tough, with leathery outer sheaths to prevent loss of moisture, and to protect the developing embryos from heat or attack. The eggs of these early reptiles contained all that their developing babies needed as they grew: a supply of food and water.

An early reptile – Sinokannemyeria

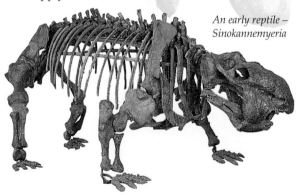

The Development of Reptiles

Just as amphibians developed from fish, so reptiles evolved from amphibians. By the Permian Period, the land was heavily colonised by non-flowering plants, many kinds of insects and a range of amphibian forms, including the giant Eryops. Now, the first reptiles appeared, and the so-called 'mammal-like reptiles', such as Moschops.

Moschops

Big Bones

At 5m (16ft 6in), Moschops was the largest of the mammal-like reptiles. Living during the late Permian Period in what is now Russia and South Africa, Moschops had a very thick, strong bone structure.

Thecodonts – Dino Ancestors

While 'mammal-like reptiles' eventually evolved into mammals, the dinosaurs evolved from reptiles similar to Euparkeria, which belonged to a group of reptiles called Thecodonts. Euparkeria probably chased insects for its food, running along quickly on its strong hind legs.

The word 'dinosaur' was first used in 1841 by Richard Owen, who was writing a report on British fossil reptiles at that time. 'Dinosaur' means 'terrible lizard'.

Painting a Dino Portrait

We know a great deal more about dinosaurs now than Richard Owen did. Dinosaur hunters have helped to paint a picture of how dinosaurs first appeared and how they evolved into familiar creatures such as Tyrannosaurus rex, Velociraptor and Triceratops. They then became extinct – quite suddenly, most scientists believe.

Ancestors You May Recognise

The thecodonts were the ancestors of dinosaurs. This same group probably also gave rise to the crocodiles, which still exist today, and the flying reptiles, the pterosaurs, which became extinct at the end of the Cretaceous Period.

Ancient crocodile skull

Herrerasaurus – Early Dinosaur

One of the first dinosaurs appeared around the Triassic Period. Herrerasaurus (Herrera's lizard) was around 3 m (10 ft) long. It had a mouth full of sharp, curved teeth. Like most early dinosaurs, it was a carnivore (meat-eater), chasing after its prey on powerful hind legs.

Rising to Power

Herrerasaurus and its kind combined the advantages of egg-laying on land, with legs placed directly under its body for easy movement. It is not surprising that dinosaurs rose quickly to power.

Speed for Survival

The earliest dinosaurs evolved in a very dangerous world. Little herbivores (plant-eaters) such as Heterodontosaurus ('different-toothed lizard') relied on speed to stay out of trouble. This gave it an advantage over the amphibians and the other much larger reptiles which existed at the same time.

Heterodontosaurus

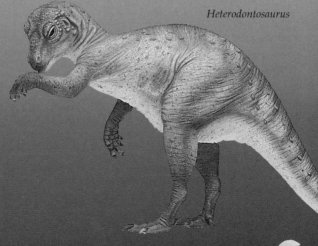

The Triassic Period marked the beginning of the Mesozoic Era, which ended with the extinction of the dinosaurs at the end of the Cretaceous Period.

The Triassic Landscape

The landscape was covered with huge conifers, giant tree-ferns and large cycads, which resembled squat palm trees. Flowering plants, broad-leaved trees and grasses had not yet evolved.

Early Appearance

The earliest dinosaurs were appearing and pterosaurs – flying reptiles – first took to the air. Dinosaurs quickly became very successful. The range of shapes, sizes and lifestyles allowed them to make the most of the conditions that existed at the time.

Plateosaurus

Long-Necked Plant-Eater

Plant-eating dinosaurs rapidly grew to great sizes. An early herbivore was Plateosaurus, which reached a length of 8 m (26 ft). This dinosaur had a long neck, enabling it to reach the tender, juicy plant tops. It probably stood on its massive hind legs.

Big Advantage

Palaeontologists – scientists who study fossils – know a lot about Plateosaurus because many fossil remains have been found. This suggests that it was a very common animal – which meant that it was a very successful one, too.

Meat-Eating Mini Monsters

There were, of course, meat-eating dinosaurs around in Triassic times, and among the most successful were small carnivores such as Coelophysis.

Coelophysis grew to around 3 m (10 ft). It was slender, long tailed, and ran on strong hind legs in pursuit of insects, lizards and smaller dinosaurs.

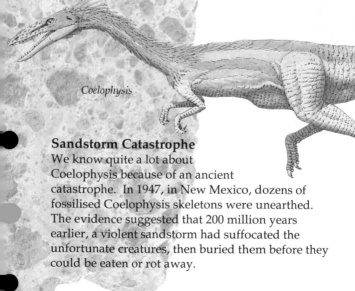

Coelophysis

Sandstorm Catastrophe

We know quite a lot about Coelophysis because of an ancient catastrophe. In 1947, in New Mexico, dozens of fossilised Coelophysis skeletons were unearthed. The evidence suggested that 200 million years earlier, a violent sandstorm had suffocated the unfortunate creatures, then buried them before they could be eaten or rot away.

The Jurassic Period was an age of great expansion for the dinosaurs. At first, plant-eating dinosaurs were mainly prosauropods – the earliest forms of what would later become the giant sauropods like Apatosaurus, and small ornithopods – the horn-beaked dinosaurs. Crocodiles, turtles and frogs flourished and pterosaurs ruled the skies.

Apatosaurus

A Changing Climate

By the end of the Jurassic Period, the Earth's original single landmass, called Pangaea, had split into two supercontinents – Laurasia in the north, and Gondwana in the south. This affected the climate, producing milder conditions and more rainfall.

The lush, tropical landscape would have included lots of ferns, and forests of giant conifers.

Late Jurassic Dinosaurs

Giant, plant-eating sauropods evolved. They would have been stalked by large, dangerous carnosaurs, such as Allosaurus (meaning 'different lizard').

Protection and Defence

Many dinosaurs had features for protection and defence. Stegosaurus ('plated reptile') had vicious-looking spikes at the end of its tail which could have inflicted a devastating wound upon any attacker.

Apatosaurus – Ground Rumbler

The giant, plant-eating sauropod, Apatosaurus, lived in late Jurassic times. Its name means 'deceptive lizard', although it was originally known as Brontosaurus, meaning 'thunder lizard'. This was because early palaeontologists thought that it must have made the ground rumble as it lumbered by!

Compsognathus – Lizard Hunter

Compsognathus

Bird-like Compsognathus also lived at this time. One of the smallest dinosaurs, it measured only 0.7 m long (2 ft 6 in) and weighed just 3 kg (6 lb 8 oz). It had a small head filled with sharp teeth, a long tail to help it balance as it ran, and short arms with two claw-tipped fingers. It was an agile hunter of insects and small lizards.

The Cretaceous Period marked the height of dinosaur development. Great and well-known dinosaurs such as T. rex, Triceratops, Gallimimus, Velociraptor, Parasaurolophus and Pachycephalosaurus all lived at this time.

A Blooming Earth

By the late Cretaceous Period, flowering plants had appeared, including trees similar to our modern beeches, maples, walnuts and oaks. The landscape would have looked more familiar to us than that of earlier times.

The Rise of the Meat-Eaters

Tyrannosaurus rex skull

The rise of the great herbivores was over. Giant plant-eaters became less common in the Cretaceous, while meat-eaters grew larger and more numerous, ending in the appearance of the fearsome tyrannosaurids, the Tyrannosaurus rex-like carnivores. All the time that this was happening, small mammals were living cautiously in the undergrowth, ready to rise to prominence once the age of the dinosaurs was over.

Troodon – 'Wounding Tooth'

Troodon was a lightly built, bird-like predator, measuring around 2 m (6 ft 6 in) long; it lived in the late Cretaceous. We can tell from its skull shape that it had a very large brain, and big eyes set forward. This meant that it had binocular vision – it could see in 3-D, as we do. It needed its big brain to process the images its eyes received as it hunted insects and small lizards. Whether it saw in colour or black-and-white is not known, but it was clearly one of the smartest dinosaurs around.

Troodon

Triceratops – Tank-Like

Triceratops was a massive, tank-like herbivore which had the longest horns of all the ceratopsians (horned dinosaurs). It weighed around 5.5 tonnes and was 9 m (30 ft) long. It was the rhinoceros of the late Cretaceous Period – although, unlike the rhino, it is now thought that Triceratops gathered into huge herds for protection.

True dinosaurs...

- had straight legs
- did not fly
- did not live in the sea

Prehistoric sea reptiles like Plesiosaurus and Icthyosaurus were not, therefore, dinosaurs.

Pterosaurs were not dinosaurs either. The most familiar one was Pterodactyl ('wing finger'), which belonged to a group called the pterodactyloids.

Pteranodon

A Crested Pterosaur

Pteranodon was another pterosaur. It sported a long, pointed head crest, which made its head, including its beak, over 1.8 m (6 ft) long. The crest probably helped to balance the long-beaked head, as the creature glided low over the sea, hunting for fish. Quetzalcoatlus was the largest ever flying reptile. It had a wingspan of 12 m (40 ft) and may have weighed around 86 kg (190 lbs).

The Flourishing Seas

Today, the largest animal that has ever lived on Earth exists in our oceans. This is the blue whale, which can be up to 34 m (111 ft) in length and weigh 200 tonnes. Before and during the age of the dinosaurs, the seas had some incredible creatures of their own. These included the plesiosaurs. Some of these marine reptiles reached 12 m (39 ft) in length. The plesiosaurs were carnivorous – they ate meat – and for most of the time they were hungry! Their prey would have included fish, each other, and icthyosaurs, another flourishing group resembling gigantic dolphins.

Plesiosaur

Here are some of the dinosaur remains which have been found around the world. Spot their location on the map opposite.

1 PACHYCEPHALOSAURUS

2 MUTTABURRASAURUS

3 COMPSOGNATHUS

4 TYRANNOSAURUS REX

5 STEGOSAURUS

6 HYPACROSAURUS

7 MAIASAURA

8 PARASAUROLOPHUS

9 GALLIMIMUS

10 MAMENCHISAURUS

11 VELOCIRAPTOR

12 TRICERATOPS

13 PROTOCERATOPS

14 HYPSILOPHODON

15 ALLOSAURUS

16 OVIRAPTOR

17 ORODROMEUS

18 APATOSAURUS

19 TROODON

20 SAUROLOPHUS

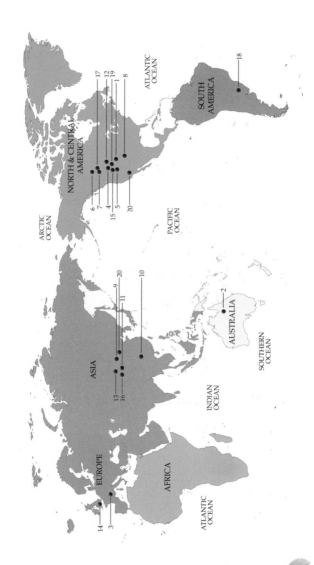

ATLANTIC
OCEAN

SOUTH
AMERICA

18

17
12
19
1
8

NORTH & CENTRAL
AMERICA

6
7
4
15
5
20

ARCTIC
OCEAN

PACIFIC
OCEAN

9
20
11
10

ASIA

13
16

AUSTRALIA

2

SOUTHERN
OCEAN

INDIAN
OCEAN

EUROPE

AFRICA

ATLANTIC
OCEAN

14
3

HOW WE KNOW ABOUT DINOSAURS

We know about dinosaurs because their remains have been found in rocks. Dinosaur hunters and scientists working in laboratories, together with artists working in studios, have pieced together bones, fragments and ground traces to create a picture of the dinosaurs and their world.

Dragon Bones

Fossil collecting is nothing new. We know that the ancient Chinese were finding dinosaur bones over 2,000 years ago – although they thought that these were the bones of huge dragons.

Even in more modern times, mistakes were made. In 1822, a dinosaur hunter named Gideon Mantell reconstructed the skeleton of a dinosaur called Iguanodon. Mantell didn't have all the pieces of this jigsaw puzzle of bones. When his reconstruction was complete, Iguanodon was displayed with a tiny horn on its nose. We now know that the 'horn' is actually Iguanodon's thumb spike, but only one of those had originally been found.

Iguanodon

HOW FOSSILS ARE FORMED

Fossils can form in many different ways. A typical example is that of the Hell Creek T. rex (see page 26), which died in or beside a river. Its flesh decayed or was eaten, leaving the bones bare. Gradually, mud and silt covered them up.

Buried and Squeezed

As years went by, the bones became buried under more mud and silt. Eventually, the bones and the mud were turned into rock.

Exposed

Over millions of years, movements of the Earth's crust brought the layers of fossil-bearing rock closer to the surface. Wind and rain eventually wore the surface rocks away, until the fossils themselves became partially exposed.

Fossil skeleton of Coelophysis

A LUCKY FIND

Dinosaurs have always fascinated and frightened us. Their popularity has helped to support expeditions and fund research projects, partly through organisations like The Dinosaur Society, which began in America.

The Hell Creek T. Rex

Sometimes, dinosaur bones are found by accident. Rancher, Kathy Wankel, was walking in the Montana Badlands when she noticed what she thought were some brownish bones poking out from a hillside. She took these fragments to a well-known palaeontologist called Jack Horner, who identified them as the bones of a T. rex. Horner knew that the area, Hell Creek, was a good place to find T. rex fossils, so in the following year, a friend of his returned to survey the site. This led to a full expedition returning to Hell Creek in 1990, where an almost complete skeleton of T. rex was unearthed.

Tyrannosaurus rex

Sometimes, before a fossil skeleton can even be seen, rocks and soil have to be dug away. In the case of the Hell Creek T. rex, portions of the hillside were removed to expose the bone-bearing rock. Then the bone surfaces were picked out using soft brushes and fine dentists' tools. Everything has to be carefully drawn, to record the precise positions of the bones.

Tools of the Trade
To remove the fossils, the team might use pneumatic drills, hammers and chisels, or very delicate blades and probes, doing as little damage as possible.

Wrapped Up
Since fossils are delicate, dinosaur hunters protect them by packing them in gauze soaked in plaster, or wrapping them in aluminium foil surrounded by a cushion of polyurethane foam. Then they are transported back to the lab.

BACK AT THE LAB

Every specimen has its packaging removed, and then the rock itself, in which the fossils are embedded. Freeing the fossils can take years of picking away with fine tools Another method is to dip the rock in an acid bath, revealing the bones within.

Dino Replicas

Because the bones are so precious, replicas are often made for reconstruction work, or to send to museums around the world. A fibreglass mould is made by using the original fossil, then lots of plaster or resin copies can be made.

Piecing It All Together

Once all the fragments have been prepared, the jigsaw can be pieced together. Palaeontologists don't just rebuild the skeleton: first they might place the fossils in a sandbox, in the positions in which they were found. This helps them to work out how the dinosaur died, and what happened to the body before it was fossilised.

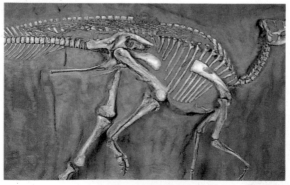

Gryposaurus skeleton

Very rarely, fossils of the soft parts of a dinosaur's body are found, but in almost all cases, experts can only base their ideas on the fossils of teeth, bones and claws.

Fossilsed Baryonyx claw

Differing Views

Early reconstructions of dinosaur skeletons reflected the general view at the time – of dinosaurs being slow, cold-blooded and rather stupid. Some modern reconstructions (which have caused great debate!) show the view of palaeontologists like Robert Bakker – that dinosaurs were active and warm-blooded.

Skeletal Clues

All modern dinosaur hunters study skeletons carefully, and from this they work out how muscles and tendons were attached. This gives a clearer idea of what the animal looked like when it was alive. Other information recorded at the site of the find – tracks and trails in the rock, for instance – provides further valuable clues about dinosaurs' lifestyles.

Fossils are usually different from original remains – chemicals have changed the remains into stone, or they have been crushed.

Different Types of Remains

Teeth: the hardest parts of all, often surviving with little change at all.

Moulds: certain minerals dissolved some bones but left bone-shaped hollow fossils called moulds.

Casts: a mould that was later filled by other minerals became a cast. Some moulds or casts can even show a dinosaur's scaly skin.

Trace fossils: other traces left by dinosaurs, including:

Ichnites: fossil footprints and fossil trackways.

Coprolites: fossilised dinosaur droppings.

Ooliths: fossilised eggs.

Iguanodon tooth

Iguanodon footprint

Gastroliths

Quite often, smooth, round, fossilised pebbles have been found with skeletons of dinosaurs such as Brachiosaurus. These pebbles, called gastroliths (gizzard stones), were deliberately swallowed by herbivores to help mash up the tough plant material that formed their diet.

Following Footprints

Fossilised tracks and trails help us to picture how dinosaurs lived. Multiple footprint tracks of Triceratops and Iguanodon, for example, help palaeontologists to work out that these and other dinosaurs were herd animals, which perhaps migrated over great distances. Scientists can also work out how fast certain dinosaurs might have moved.

The big herbivores seemed to have lumbered along slowly, while small predatory carnivores, on the other hand, zoomed along in search of prey – or avoided being eaten themselves.

Iguanodon foot bones

Brachiosaurus

COLOURFUL OR DRAB?

Some books picture dinosaurs in very drab colours – dull greens, greys or browns – but a number of palaeontologists think that at least some dinosaurs might have been very brightly coloured indeed.

Distinctive Markings

Vivid colours are common in animals today. Just think about the markings of hummingbirds, butterflies or lizards.

Modern-day lizard

Colouring and markings are used for several purposes, identification and display being two of the most important. If you want to attract a mate, you need to stand out in the crowd – but at the same time you want to let others know that you belong to the crowd. Colours help you do that. They also act as warnings, so that predators will think twice before attacking.

AMBER AND DNA

Amber is the fossilised resin of certain trees. Sometimes, insects got covered in resin and became fossilised, too. Excitement has been generated by the idea that fossilised mosquitoes might have had a meal of dinosaur blood just before they died in the amber. This means that the dinosaur blood would also have been preserved.

To Make a Dinosaur...

All cells contain a substance called DNA, which holds the genetic instructions for making a complete individual. Some people think that it just might be possible, if enough fossilised DNA can be gathered, to piece together the instructions for making a dinosaur.

Insect trapped in amber

Could it Work?

The great difficulty is that DNA is fragile and easily damaged. Also, even the most recent dinosaur DNA is 65 million years old. Many, scientists think that it will never be possible to grow a dinosaur...not that this will stop people trying, of course.

Dinosaur fossils are fragile, but fossilised eggs and the bones of baby dinosaurs are especially delicate.

Many of the dinosaurs lived in wet lowlands, so if the babies died, their delicate bones would have rotted away quickly, before they could become fossilised. The best finds are of babies and nests from dry upland areas, where the remains were better protected.

Eating the Evidence

Although some dinosaur parents cared for their young, many eggs and hatchlings would have fallen prey to hungry carnivores, which gobbled them up! This is another reason why finds of dinosaur babies are limited.

Lots of Herbivores

The finest and biggest finds of fossil eggs and nestlings are those of Protoceratops and Maiasaura, both herbivores. Herbivores were much more common than carnivores, so there are more of their bones to be found.

Protoceratops hatchlings

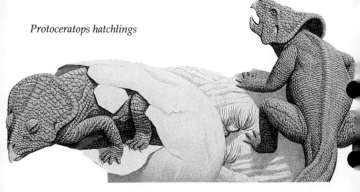

Tough Shells to Crack

Dinosaur eggs had harder shells than those laid by their ancestors. The tough, chalky outer shell not only protected the embryo developing inside, it also prevented water loss. An egg is really a self-contained environment – a little world where the baby dinosaur prepared itself for survival.

Fossilised Protoceratops eggs

Sunny Side Up?

Like birds' eggs today, a dinosaur's egg contained a yolk – the food supply of the embryo – and an albumen, or egg white, which was a cushioning fluid between the embryo and the shell.

Protective Membranes

Further protection was provided by three membranes surrounding the baby dinosaur. The 'chorion' lined the inner surface of the shell. The 'allantois' enclosed a sac which contained the embryo's waste products; it also carried oxygen to the embryo. The inner membrane, the 'amnion', formed a cushion around the embryo itself.

Dinosaur embryo

Dinosaur eggs varied in size depending on how big the adult animals were, although most dinosaur eggs were relatively small compared to the size of the parents.

Hypselosaurus – Big Eggs

One of the largest eggs ever found measured 30 cm (12 in) by 25 cm (10 in), and had a capacity of 3.3 litres (nearly 6 pts) – that's twice the size of a modern ostrich egg! Dinosaur hunters think that it belonged to a large herbivore called Hypselosaurus (meaning 'high ridge lizard'). No egg much larger than this could ever have hatched successfully. Hypselosaurus' eggs probably weighed around 7 kilos (15 lbs 7 oz). If they had any larger and heavier, the shells would have cracked; or the weight of fluid inside might have suffocated the embryo. Oxygen could not have passed through the thick shell to the embryo, and the hatchling would certainly have struggled to break out.

Ostrich egg

NESTLINGS

The nestlings of some modern-day birds are very poorly developed. They have hardly any feathers, their eyes are closed, and they need constant care. Other kinds of nestlings are well developed. Their bodies have down, their eyes are open, and they can walk straight away.

By studying the fossil skeletons of dinosaur hatchlings, palaeontologists think that these differences applied in prehistoric times, too.

Maiasaura – 'Good Mother Lizard'

In the late Cretaceous Period, there was a dinosaur called Maiasaura. It was a hadrosaur – a duck-billed, plant-eating dinosaur – and it built great nests measuring around 3 m (10 ft) in diameter. Maiasaura was large, but its hatchlings were small and poorly developed. They could only have survived by staying in the nest, and being constantly cared for.

Maiasaura

Palaeontologists can't always gain a clear picture of what dinosaurs were like, or how they behaved, from the fossil evidence. A useful way of learning more is to make comparisons with creatures living today.

In order to understand more about dinosaur eggs and nesting sites, scientists sometimes look at the way modern crocodiles bring up their young, as crocodiles are related to dinosaurs.

Crocodile Parenting

A female crocodile lays her eggs in the warm mud of the river bank. When the young begin to hatch out, she helps them from their shells and carries them to the water. She guards them fiercely, until they are large and strong enough to look after themselves. Palaeontologists believe that dinosaurs cared for their young in a similar way.

Modern young crocodile

How Do They Know?

Experts can't be absolutely sure that some dinosaurs looked after their young. However, they can put together the pieces of the jigsaw puzzle that they have, and guess what the rest of the picture was like.

For example, one dinosaur of the late Cretaceous Period was Hypacrosaurus (meaning 'nearly the highest lizard') – a large herbivore. It had no natural defences – no horns like Triceratops or tail spikes like Stegosaurus; it must have relied upon its keen senses.

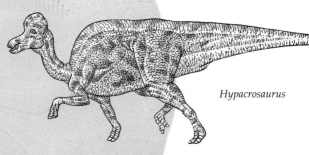

Hypacrosaurus

Adult Hypacrosaurus used their sharp senses to guard their young as well as themselves. The babies were no bigger than a small dog, and if the parents had not guarded them from predators, Hypacrosaurus would quickly have become extinct!

Before the first Maiasaura nests were found, scientists thought that female dinosaurs left their babies to hatch out and take care of themselves. Now they know that this was not the case.

Dinosaur Nursery

When dinosaur hunters discovered the first Maiasaura nests in 1979, they were astonished to find so many in one place. Each nest would have been scooped out of the sandy ground by a female adult, then lined with soft plants, to make a soft cushion. She then laid 18 to 30 eggs, and possibly squatted over them or piled plants on top, to help them incubate.

Baby Teeth

The fossil skeletons of the hatchlings show that some had worn teeth. This suggests that they ate tough plant food brought to them by their parents.

Maiasaura nests

A Recent Find

Maiasaura eggs have only been found fairly recently. As have the nest sites of a plant-eater called Orodromeus (meaning 'mountain runner'), which lived at the same time.

Orodromeus hatchlings were born fully formed and able to forage for themselves, but their parents probably stayed near, to protect and care for them.

Orodromeus hatchlings

The First Eggs

Dinosaur eggs were first found in 1923, in Mongolia's Gobi Desert. They belonged to a tiny ceratopsian named Protoceratops (meaning 'first horned face').

Since then, many Protoceratops nesting sites have been discovered, together with fossil skeletons showing all stages of the animal's development.

EVIDENCE OF DANGER

Carnivores got their food when they could. They hunted actively some of the time, and probably scavenged carcasses, too. Some also tried to steal the eggs of other dinosaurs.

Oviraptor – 'Egg Thief'

Oviraptor was well-adapted for egg stealing. Slim and agile, it could dart quickly into a nest site and carry an egg away in its strong, grasping claws.

Nifty Egg Crackers

The front of Oviraptor's beak was toothless, but it had two bony prongs jutting down from the roof of its mouth. These were used for cracking open the stolen eggs so that the hungry beast could gulp up the tasty insides.

Oviraptor

Caught Red-Handed

Oviraptor fossils have been found in Mongolia. A skull and skeleton were found lying on top of a nest full of Protoceratops' eggs. Caught in the act by an angry parent?

A Herd of Footprints

A site in Winston, Queensland, Australia, shows the footprints of a 150-strong herd of dinosaurs, and those of a solitary carnivore. It was opened as a public national park in 1982. Here is what may have happened there millions of years ago...

A Quick Drink

A herd of plant-eating dinosaurs stopped at a lake to drink. Some of them kept watch, because danger was always present. Even so, they were taken by surprise when a large carnivore charged from the undergrowth.

The Attack

The herd stampeded, some of them splashing into the water, others darting for cover. With a great roar, the meat-eater attacked one of the slower herbivores.

A Mystery

Did the predator catch its lunch? We'll never know! Only the footprints remain...nothing more.

At the end of the Cretaceous Period, around 65 million years ago, dinosaurs became extinct, together with icthyosaurs, plesiosaurs, pterosaurs, and many other species. But what caused this disaster?

Icthyosaurus

Just Too Big?

Early ideas included the notion that dinosaurs died out because they became too big and bulky for their own good. Because it was known that small prehistoric mammals existed, some people suggested that these had attacked and eaten dinosaur eggs, causing dinosaur extinction.

Food Poisoning

At this time, flowering plants were appearing on Earth. If these new species proved poisonous to herbivores, the whole food chain could have been disastrously affected.

Suffocated

One theory, with lots of good evidence, is that intense volcanic activity poisoned the atmosphere, upsetting the balance of the environment. Certainly, vast chains of volcanoes were erupting for thousands of years. These volcanoes would have dumped enormous quantities of carbon dioxide into the atmosphere, and this might well have caused enough damage to start the dinosaur extinction.

Devastating Meteorite

The other main theory is that a large meteorite from space smashed into the Earth, causing the same kind of devastation and atmospheric pollution as volcanic eruptions. In recent years, the remains of a huge crater have been detected off the Yucatan Peninsula in Mexico. It is the right size and age to have been responsible for the extinction of all the dinosaurs.

Dinosaurs roamed the Earth for around 160 million years, changing and adapting to fit into their world. If they had not become extinct, they would have continued to evolve. However, it would be wrong to think that T. rex, Triceratops, Stegosaurus and others would have survived unchanged to the modern day.

A Common Myth

Some films and fiction books show dinosaurs living at the same time as primitive cavemen, which is quite wrong. Over 60 million years went by after the death of the dinosaurs before anything like a human arrived on the scene!

Dinosaurs Move Over

We must not forget that it was the dinosaur extinction that allowed mammals to take over... and that includes us. If dinosaurs were still around, we probably wouldn't be.

The earliest mammals appeared in the Triassic Period, when dinosaurs were going strong. But dinosaurs were so successful that mammals remained small and in the background.

Natural Successors

Mammals were the ideal successors to the dinosaurs. They were warm-blooded, they had active lifestyles, they were inquisitive, and they had large brains relative to their body size. Mammals also had live young and often had complicated social structures.

It's a Mammal's World

Since Cretaceous times, mammals have spread throughout the world and flourished. After 65 million years of evolution, mammals have developed into whales, elephants, lions, bats, cats, dogs and horses...the list goes on.

Hyracotherium – earliest ancestor of the horse

ARE ALL DINOSAURS EXTINCT?

Strictly speaking, all dinosaurs are extinct. Despite some wild stories about sightings of sauropod-like dinosaurs in African lakes, palaeontologists are pretty certain that dinosaurs as we know them are not alive today.

However, it has been known for some time that Archaeopteryx, the so-called 'first bird', bore many similarities to the small theropod ('beast-footed') dinosaurs such as Velociraptor, Compsognathus and Troodon. This has made many scientists think that birds evolved from dinosaurs.

Archaeopteryx

Because of these facts, and other pieces of evidence, many scientists have suggested that birds have evolved from the dinosaurs, and remain their closest living relatives.